Mysteries Over Georgia

Erin Cain

Published by Erin Cain, 2024.

MYSTERIES OVER GEORGIA

First edition. May 10, 2024.

ISBN: 979-8224841059

Written by Erin Cain.

Table of Contents

To my fellow Georgians.

Preface

The following newspaper articles elucidate a series of unexplained or rare occurrences in the skies over Georgia. Some of these events may have had natural explanations that were unknown to their witnesses. Efforts have been made to eliminate reports that coincide with known meteor showers, comets, and other documented phenomena.

It's important to note that some of the language used in these articles is outdated. I have corrected spelling errors and archaic spellings to ensure readability. However, I have chosen not to remove offensive language. Doing so would not alter the underlying tone of disdain for the Black population, the perception of Black people as foolish and superstitious, or the casual dismissal of reports from Black witnesses. Instead of focusing on the prejudice commonplace in that era, I encourage you to read between the lines to see the underlying information in these accounts.

Chapter 1: Mystery Airships

3

June 1897
Atlanta, Fulton County, Capital Region

June 11, 1897 - The Constitution (Atlanta, Fulton County, GA)

AN AIR SHIP THIS, OR A STRAY COMET?

A Strange Light Seen in the Southeast Just Before Day.

MANY ATLANTIANS VIEW IT

They Say It Has the Brilliance of a Powerful Electric Lamp.

CARRIES PORT AND STARBOARD LIGHTS

A Reputable Witness Noticed It Lurch To One Side—Hotel Guests Awakened and Watched It Closely.

Have you seen the brilliant air ship?

It swings every clear morning in the eastern horizon. It has mystified many intelligent men and caused those of a superstitious tendency to open their eyes in awe.

A light has arisen in the east, a very mysterious light. Whether it is an air ship or whether it be some strange atmospheric phenomenon, or some unknown glory of the heavens, no one can say, but it has been named the air ship and not less than 100 reputable Atlantians have seen it.

Those who chanced to be awake at the early hour yesterday morning and beheld the strange sight talked little else all day.

The strange light was first discovered Sunday morning, when the night watchman of the Kimball ran down stairs to notify the night clerk that an air ship was crossing the horizon. An alarm was then raised and at least half a hundred people saw what was supposed to be the empyrean navigator.

Yesterday morning it appeared again about 3 o'clock and with those who saw it, and some of them were men of more than ordinary intelligence, it caused a great wonderment.

The light is described as being very brilliant. It is almost due southeast of Atlanta and it is several degrees above the horizon.

Here is the way it is described by one of the best known men in Atlanta.

"I was in my room at the Kimball when the night watchman knocked and asked if I wanted to see the air ship. I went at once and when I climbed out on the parapet the first thing that struck my gaze was this peculiar light. The city was studded at the time with electric lights. This strange sight in the heavens was more than I could understand. It had the brilliance of an electric light and it shone with powerful effect. The heavens were painted with the pale green cast which comes just before the breaking of day—that strange, indescribable color which great artists have so often strived for.

"It appeared to me that there were three lights in a horizontal line. At one time it seemed that they gave a great lurch and I can readily understand how the thing, whatever it is, can be called an air ship. It is not Venus nor any of the planets. I am versed enough in astronomy to tell that it was none of the constellations. Behind the great white light could be seen now and then the stars themselves like needle points. It gave me an uncanny feeling. I have talked of it to no one and had rather than you would not use my name as I don't care to be questioned too much about it."

Night Clerk Joe Raine, of the Kimball, saw the light Sunday morning.

It was the same that appeared yesterday.

"It was very low when I first saw it," said Mr. Raine, "and I could see only a ruddy glare above the horizon. Soon it appeared to view and I could readily see the bright light which the so-called air ship carried. It resembled a huge arc light with three times the power of those in ordinary use and gave forth a light of dazzling whiteness almost as trying as calcium light. There were intermittent flashes like the passing of a spark of some powerful electric current.

"About the light was the dim outline of what appeared to be a bulky object. It may have been imagination which painted this, but it gave every appearance of being an air ship."

Night Watchman Scott, of the Kimball, and a number of policemen and others who were up at that time of the morning gave practically the same account.

What the mysterious light of the heavens is no one seems to know.

Should it be clear this morning it will be viewed by hundreds who have heard of it.

June 14, 1897 - The Constitution (Atlanta, Fulton County, GA)

THEY DISCUSS THE AIRSHIP.

Strange Light in the East Is Interesting to Stargazers.

The mysterious airship still hovers in the eastern sky. Every day new witnesses are added to the already long list of those who have seen the aerial craft. Hitherto skeptical Atlantians are rapidly falling into line, and the city's population is fast being divided into two classes—those who have seen the airship and those who have not.

The latest prominent citizen upon whose astonished vision it has burst is Mr. E. P. Chamberlin.

Mr. Chamberlin has seen the much talked of object a number of times recently, always at the same hour, shortly before sunrise, and always to the northeast of the city.

He, however, does not subscribe to the airship theory by any means. In his opinion, the strange, luminous body is an enormous meteor falling through the immensity of space towards the earth's surface. The object, he says, has appeared nearer and nearer every time he has seen it.

Mr. Chamberlin is confident that he has arrived at the correct solution of the mystery and he is by no means alone in this belief. Several other people have been earnestly scrutinizing the eastern skies every morning about daybreak and their observations have brought them to a similar conclusion.

Others there are who claim to have seen the supposed airship or meteor and to have recognized it as nothing more than a small patch of clouds glowing in the first beams of the rising sun.

Not the least remarkable part of the very remarkable affair is the large number of people whom it has proven to be up and star-gazing as a regular thing between 3 and 4 o'clock in the mornings. Atlantians have always been known as an uncommonly wide-awake people, but the airship excitement has revolutionized all previous ideas as to the extent of that quality among them.

June 1897
Eastman, Dodge County, South Georgia

June 18, 1897 - The Times-Journal (Eastman, Dodge County, GA)

The Airship.

Mr. B. T. Burch, one of our most reliable citizens, states that on Tuesday morning last about three o'clock he saw what was clearly to his mind the airship which has been much talked of of late.

He says that he saw a light in the heavens going in an easterly direction which looked very much like the headlight of a locomotive and it remained in sight for about an hour—during which time it reversed itself several times.

Mr. Burch's statement has caused considerable excitement and some of our citizens are watching nightly for a reappearance of the ship.

June 1897
Wolf Pit, Bacon County, South Georgia

June 24, 1897 - The Fitzgerald Leader (Fitzgerald, Irwin County, GA)

Several people saw a strange light last Wednesday night in the heavens and did not know what caused it. But we are of the opinion it was a meteor or that stray air ship that has been seen in the different parts of the country lately, causing so much comment through the leading papers of the country. It may be the ship that was stolen from Esquire Hoffman and Co. at Roana, Ind., who made a trip to the North Pole early in the spring, and after they came back the ship was stolen from the company.

July 1907
Decatur, DeKalb County, Capital Region

July 15, 1907 - The Atlanta Journal (Atlanta, Fulton County, GA)

PHANTOM BALLOON SPEEDS OVER DECATUR

CITIZENS SAY A MYSTERIOUS LIGHTED BODY PASSED ABOVE TOWN AT TWILIGHT ON SUNDAY

Just at nightfall Sunday a number of people in Decatur were astounded by the appearance of a great light in the sky, seemingly a mammoth balloon or airship, that sped high above the town, going in a northeasterly direction. For ten minutes, it is said, the mysterious body was visible. Then it vanished in a mass of gathering clouds.

Among those who witnessed the marvel was W. H. Christian, whose home is on the western edge of the village. From where he stood, says Mr. Christian, the light looked pretty much as might a comet upside down. The upper part of the queer air craft seemed to be an enormous bag that fluttered like silk in the atmospheric currents. Whether there was a parachute or boat of some kind attached to this, the distance of the moving body made it impossible to determine. For the same reason, too, it is not known whether the bag was guided by a human hand or moved of its own accord.

That it was under intelligent direction, however, the steadiness and straightness with which it kept its course is strongly suggestive. A carrier pigeon, say the witnesses, never moved with more precision.

Who first sighted the phenomenon is not known, but shortly after its appearance scores of people were calling to each other and pointing toward the sky. Had it not been for the fact that most families were having supper at the time the excitement would have been much greater than it really was. Excitement was not lacking, however. Among the animals, the effect of the balloon was striking. Dogs yowled and howled, cats went scampering up trees and under houses, the chicken roosts became a pandemonium.

So far as is known no one in Atlanta saw the light. This is easily understood, however, for, according to Mr. Christian, the body swept into view about five miles northeast of the city.

Much speculation has been aroused over what may be called this phantom flyer. No aeronauts have been scheduled to make ascensions, and if a comet was due, the almanacs and astronomers have kept quiet on the subject.

July 1909
Atlanta, Fulton County, Capital Region

July 28, 1909 - The Atlanta Journal (Atlanta, Fulton County, GA)

WAS IT AN AIRSHIP FLYING OVER ATLANTA?

Strange Light in Eastern Sky on Tuesday Night Attracted Interesting Attention

People in the neighborhood of West Peachtree place and Spring street were startled last night about 10 o'clock to see a strange and brilliant light in the eastern heavens. It was first noticed by a family who were gathered on the front veranda enjoying the cool evening breezes. They called the attention of their neighbors to it, and it was soon causing no little commotion in the community.

The light glowed with a peculiar reddish brilliancy different to a star, and was considerably larger. Some thought it was surely an airship, and the light was its danger signals, which it carried before and aft to avoid collision with any other air craft which might be floating about in these flighty times or stray and unknown planets which might be encountered. Others were certain it must be a comet or meteor.

It appeared to be a long ways off when first discovered, and seemed traveling in an eastern direction and gradually grew dimmer. Finally, all discussion and conjecture on the subject was cut short by the light suddenly disappearing as mysteriously as it had appeared, leaving the gazers speechless with wonder and amazement. There will be quite a crowd on the lookout for it this evening.

October 1910
Atlanta, Fulton County, Capital Region

Oct 30, 1910 - The Ledger (Columbus, Muskogee County, GA)

Phantom Airship Has Been Seen Again

Atlanta, Ga., Oct. 29.-It has been seen again.

Yes, that phantom airship with red storm-lights which created such a stir in Atlanta last winter has again been sighted by people coming home from their clubs at midnight.

Yesterday somebody called up all the newspaper offices to tell them the airship was in full sight in the west. But it wasn't even a hot-air balloon—just plain hot air, without any bag around it.

June 1911
Atlanta, Fulton County, Capital Region

June 11, 1911 - The Atlanta Journal (Atlanta, Fulton County, GA)

MYSTERY IN SKY KEPT ATLANTIANS GUESSING

What was it.

Atlanta sat up and guessed, but nobody answered.

Nobody yet knows what it was that went flying over or beyond the western portion of the city yesterday afternoon about 3:30 o'clock.

Hundreds saw it from the streets. Forsyth street and the plaza of the Terminal station offered exceptionally good vantage points for watching it float across the sky. They were nearly congested with watchers.

It might have been a quarter of a mile away. It might have been half a mile away. It might have been a whole mile, or even farther.

Nobody identified it, and consequently nobody could guess how big it ought to be close at hand or how far it was away from their own eyes. Nobody was certain whether it was a balloon or an air ship or a heat wave or a cyclone, or what.

The only thing that everybody knew was that it was something real, for everybody saw it at once. It wasn't any highly individualized case of [?], or anything like that. It was the real goods, whatever its gender or religious persuasion or other dimension might be.

One man stepped off the door sill of a near-beer joint on Forsyth street and nearly broke his neck before he regained his balance. Then he saw it. He straightened stiff and stared at it, first with one eye, then with the other, then with both together. Then he turned and marched steadily back into the saloon.

A visitor who had just come in on a train at the Terminal found everybody staring into the air beyond his head when he emerged upon the plaza. He started and walked stiff-necked straight ahead, with a smile that meant, "You can't catch me." When he stepped up on the corner of the curb at Mitchell street and Madison avenue he heard some one say "air ship." He was still rubbering when the speck disappeared.

All sorts of conjectures were offered as to what the thing was. It might have been a foreign air ship taking a bird's-eye view of Atlanta's battle for commission government. It might have been the weather man getting safely out of town before sweltering Atlantians could lay their hands on him today. It might have been Dr. Cook.

It might even have been the famed Atlanta spirit taking wings in flight. But no.

It might have been anything. It was surely something. Pay your money and make your guess.

September 1915
Atlanta, Fulton County, Capital Region

Sept 19, 1915 - The Atlanta Journal (Atlanta, Fulton County, GA)

Airship Reported Seen Flying Over Atlanta by Night

The mysterious airship! The boys of Bellwood have seen it rushing through the night, they have heard the beating of its wings at dawn and followed the soaring flash of its headlight into the darkness.

Whence it comes or whither it goes, whether the secret flight of a recluse inventor or a bird of a more sinister omen, they do not know, nor have all their efforts to trace it to the canebrakes along the Chattahoochee river discovered the slightest clue.

But that it is an airship and that for a week past it has swept over Bellwood between dusk and daylight, a dozen of them are ready to declare. And their fathers, too, say they have watched the spears of light, like the fingers of the Midnight Sun, gleam and glow and fade to nothing in the sky.

They are all very excited about it and while jokes about Zeppelins are many of course, there is a real and keen desire to trace the lights and the wing-beats and the bulk of black to their origin.

Alton Bartlett, a youth who lives on Center Hill avenue, is said to have seen the airship first when he was driving a mule into Atlanta about 3 o'clock last Thursday morning. He told The Journal he heard the whirr of the propellers and looked up in time to glimpse a great shadow close to the tops of the trees and what looked like the figure of a man crouched in the center of it all. Then the light from the peak of the airship blinded him and swept on and he looked again to see it vanish into the darkness to the west and the light die out.

Ben Burton, another Center Hill boy, says he was awakened in the middle of the night by the whirring noise, and others among their friends and neighbors claim to have heard it and seen the strange flashes in the sky.

October 1915
Americus, Sumter County, Southwest Georgia

Oct 18, 1915 - The Americus Daily Times-Recorder (Americus, Sumter County, GA)

The same mysterious airship was seen passing over Americus and duly chronicled by this paper several weeks ago. Its voyage along this way was timed after midnight, and several late schooners caught sight of it as it passed over the Americus bar.

Chapter 2: Balls of Fire

May 1858
Haywood Valley, Chattooga County, Northwest Georgia

May 10, 1858 - The Daily Sun (Columbus, Muskogee County, GA)

Wonderful Phenomenon.

We learn from Mr. A. P. Smith, of N. C., that a strange light was seen in Haywood Valley, Chattooga co., last Saturday night at about nine o'clock. Mr. S. was on a visit to his brother, David Smith, and, at the time the light appeared, was sitting out at the door, with several friends in conversation. Suddenly the darkness became illuminated so intensely as to give well defined shadows to isolated objects around, and enabled them to see better than by the light of a full moon. Upon looking they saw what appeared to be a globe of fire at a distance of between one quarter and half a mile, about the size of a half bushel measure, from forty to sixty feet above the ground, of a beautiful brilliancy, very much resembling the head light of a locomotive, but much more intense. This light continued for about half an hour, gently moving up and down having no motion in a horizontal direction. From this strange globe of fire little balls were continually shooting up and descending in parabolic curves much resembling miniature sky rockets. After about half an hour this wonderful light rapidly diminished, and after a few flickerings, entirely disappeared.—Rome Courier.

March 1879
Alapaha, Berrien County, South Georgia

Mar 14, 1879 - The Oglethorpe Echo (Crawford, Oglethorpe County, GA)

The Berrien County News has information of a ghost or some other mysterious apparition. It says: "On last Sunday night, as Captain Austin and Mr. J. A. Slater were returning from church, they beheld a strange phenomenon, in the shape of a ball of fire, about the size of a half bushel measure. When first seen it was near the earth, and about five or six hundred yards distant from them. It rose rapidly until it attained a height of fifty feet, when it took a northerly course and traveled at the rate of about twenty miles an hour. After going in that direction for perhaps a quarter of a mile it turned suddenly and came back to where it started. When it arrived over the place where it was first seen, it began a vibratory motion and continued for a few moments, when it fell to the earth and became extinct. The light from this strange body was of a pale, whitish color. Our informant assures us that, at a distance of six or eight hundred yards, the light from it plainly revealed the rough bark on the pine trees as it passed."

March 1883
Americus, Sumter County, Southwest Georgia

Mar 30, 1883 - The Savannah Morning News (Savannah, Chatham County, GA)

A strange story was told a day or two since by a countryman living in the vicinity of Americus. He said that a ball of fire suddenly sprang up before him on the public road while he was on his way home, keeping steadily before him until opposite a graveyard, when it turned and rested in mid air over that burial place. He said that he was so badly frightened that he was out of breath from running when he got home.

May 1888
Dalton, Whitfield County, Northwest Georgia

May 3, 1888 - The Citizen (Dalton, Whitfield County, GA)

A strange light was seen in the sky a few nights ago by several persons. The appearance of the light resembled a huge wheel of fire, revolving rapidly as it shot athwart the heavens. It was probably a large aerolite.

October 1895
Albany, Dougherty County, Southwest Georgia

Oct 27, 1895 - The Morning News (Savannah, Chatham County, GA)

BALLS OF FIRE IN THE ROAD.

A Strange Phenomenon Reported in Dougherty County.

Albany, Ga., Oct. 26.—Last night a strange phenomenon presented itself to a party of young ladies and gentlemen of this city, who went to a dance in the eastern section of the county. Several times during the journey to and from the dance balls of fire springing from tiny sparks would gather together and dash under and around their vehicles, in many instances brilliantly illuminating the surroundings and badly frightening the horses and superstitious of the party. A gentleman of Harrall county [Note: There is no Harrall County in Georgia. This is most likely Haralson, but could also be Harris.] who is down in this section selling his crop of apples, had the same experience between this city and Dawson a few nights ago. As he was driving leisurely along in his covered wagon, two immense balls of fire seemed to rise as if by magic and roll across the road underneath the feet of the horses. So sudden and unexpected was the phenomenon that the team came near running away and tearing up the wagon.

1910 and Thirty Years Previous
Dyas, Monroe County, Central Georgia

Apr 1, 1910 - The Jackson Argus (Jackson, Butts County, GA)

The people of Dyas, a small village in the western part of Monroe county, are greatly puzzled over a strange and most wonderful phenomena that makes its nightly appearance on the plantation of Mr. James Holloway, one of the most prominent citizens and farmers of that vicinity. It generally makes its appearance about 11 o'clock at night, and can be seen from that time until day breaks, when it disappears. It is said that it has existed for thirty years or more, and during that time has been seen by hundreds of people. The writer was told about the phenomena by Mr. Lamar Smith, a highly respected citizen of Forsyth. No matter, according to investigations, what is the nature of the weather, whether it is hot or cold, whether it is raining, snowing or sleeting, it makes its appearance almost every night in the year, and is certainly the most supernatural occurrence, the most wonderful phenomena, in the history of Monroe or probably any other county in the State. It is a source of the greatest bewilderment to those who have seen it. It is said to resemble a small globule of fire about the size of a baseball, and although it is very bright, like the light of a lamp, it does not cast any reflection, and is not illuminating. It generally remains about thirty feet above the earth and constantly travels over a sixteen-acre field near the residence of Mr. Holloway. Sometimes it dances along the ground. Many desperate attempts have been made by the citizens of Dyas to get close enough to the object to ascertain the nature of the phenomena, but as one gradually nears it it suddenly disappears and makes its appearance again at a distance. It has been seen by many of the most prominent and influential citizens of Monroe county, men whose veracity cannot be questioned, and who have frequently stated that they would make affidavits to the effect that they had seen the phenomena and that it is certainly the most wonderful occurrence they have ever witnessed. They state that it is not a jack-o'-lantern, as the field where it makes its appearance is located at a high altitude, where there is no vapor, and that it is not phosphorus, because they cannot approach it.

Paul Russell Williams.

February 1912
Atlanta, Fulton County, Capital Region

Feb 22, 1912 - The Dalton Citizen (Dalton, Whitfield County, GA)

Ball of Fire.

The recurring appearance in the negro section of Atlanta of a strange ball of rolling fire, which has been seen by hundreds of white people as well as negroes, has terribly frightened some of the colored people of the community, and has aroused others to heights of religious zeal that amount almost to frenzy.

The rolling ball of fire, which is said to measure four or five feet in circumference, has been seen principally in a low section of the city, where the mists hang heavy at night, and local scientists have expressed the opinion that it was probably some kind of "fox-fire" or some electrical phenomenon, but the negroes believe it portends the end of the world.

Others of the negroes claim to believe that it is the old Biblical pillar of fire that led the Children of Israel by day as they marched out of Egyptian bondage, and they say that the sign has come anew to mark the regeneration of the negro race.

March 1914
Valdosta, Lowndes County, South Georgia

Mar 27, 1914 - The Valdosta Daily Times (Valdosta, Lowndes County, GA)

Huge Ball Of Light Is Seen In The East By Valdosta Folks

A great ball of light, which flashed across the eastern sky late Thursday afternoon, caused much speculation in Valdosta, and almost resulted in a panic in the negro districts.

The phenomenon occurred about 6.30 o'clock and was witnessed by a number of people. The light, which resembled a flash like an explosion, lasted for only a few seconds, but it illuminated the entire sky.

The light traveled from north to south and left no trail behind it. A number of persons who saw the light said that it suddenly flared up and then died away as quickly as it came.

Others said that the light had the appearance of a ball of fire and seemed to be from eight to twelve feet in circumference.

Chapter 3: Spook Lights

31

November 1878
Columbus, Muskogee County, West Georgia

Nov 23, 1878 - The Columbus Daily Times (Columbus, Muskogee County, GA)

A Strange Hallucination

A Veritable Fata Morgana at the Old Brickyard

Probable Effects of a Dose of Early Rising

Although the wise Solomon remarked some few thousand years ago that "there is nothing new under the sun," and, with due respect to the wise King, as things will occasionally happen that seem to contradict this famous dictum, the chronicler of the succeeding event may be pardoned by the kind readers of the Times for its reproduction.

Early yesterday morning, when darkness still reigned supreme, and the effulgent rays of the day illuminator were still hid by the sable folds of night, one of Columbus' enterprising young men arose with the laudable determination to kill a few nice, fat ducks for his breakfast, possibly his dinner—we are not certain at this point.

En passant it may be said that this is a good season for ducks, the weather of the past week having contributed wonderfully to the aquatic life of the duck. The ducks enjoy it, that kind of weather. Our hero wanted to enjoy the ducks. He is a thoughtful fellow and up to snuff, as the lingo goeth. Well, we said our hero arose; yes, and he dressed himself to suit the emergency, and charging a trusted gun with lots of ammunition, he sailed forth into the cold night air. Whew! how the cold wind whistled and made him shiver. It still lacked a couple of hours before sunrise would deign to smile upon the denizens of this vale of—disappointment.

But our hero is as brave as he is handsome.

Undaunted and with a gleeful stride he briskly stepped away 'till he reached the proposed scene of action—the old brickyard. But it was yet too dark to see; the objects around our doughty hunter were scarcely to be distinguished.

But then, kind reader, please bear in mind that the hero of this occurrence also possesses the very enviable virtue of patience (he is neither an editor nor proof reader.) So he patiently waited for day and the ducks.

While thus pleasantly engaged, speculating perhaps on the probable luck he was going to encounter, his attention was suddenly drawn towards a large moving light, away in the East. The light looked bright, white and queer—the expectant slayer of the ducks was sorely puzzled.

It somewhat resembled the headlight of a moving locomotive, but while consoling himself with this comforting reflection, the strange Phenomenon moved onwards, upwards, higher and higher. It got far about the horizon and it reminded him on an illuminated balloon by its risings and diffings. And stranger still, it oscillated from the right to the left, and again from the left hand to the right. Intently, eagerly did our young man observe the bright light—its movements were ever strange and on the hob goblin order. Then he fell into a deep rumination—that lasted a while. Then he looked up again and lo! he discovered—what do you suppose, oh! patient reader—the moon. That was too much. He staggered under the weight of conflicting emotions, and "silently stole away." But our friend is also a cautious man. So, on his way home, he called the attention of several early risers whom he met by chance, to this passing strange freak in mother nature's well regulated household. He stoutly in common with others asserts the truth of this strange face, and as he is also a truthful man, we have no reason to doubt the tale and also because "truth is stranger far than fiction."

We solemnly enquired whether he had mixed anything with his early coffee, but no, that was not done.

And inasmuch as our very good friend and well-wisher—the hero of this unvarnished tale—did bring no ducks to his "Duck," we can not furnish our kind readers with a solution of this fata morganatic story.

June 1890
Atlanta, Fulton County, Capital Region

June 16, 1890 - The Constitution (Atlanta, Fulton County, GA)

A Strange Light.

Last night a mysterious light was observed by many citizens passing over Atlanta from the western to the eastern horizon. It appeared about the size of a gas-jet flame, and beamed brightly, even in the clouds that obscured the horizon. No one knew what it was, but the general belief was that it was a toy balloon carrying a candle. It created a small sensation as it slowly passed over the city and went down in the western suburbs.

June 1892
Sheffield, Rockdale County, Capital Region

June 18, 1892 - Hale's Weekly (Conyers, Rockdale County, GA)

Mr. J. L. Shaw, a very well known young man in our community, was out at a late hour last Sunday night. He said there was a mysterious light shone out right around him of which he couldn't account for. He said he "shore hit it" for a mile and a half.

December 1893
Waycross, Ware County, Southeast Georgia

12, 1893 - The Morning News (Savannah, Chatham County, GA)

Alvin Johnson, son of Capt. L. Johnson, says that he saw a strange sight at the Kettle Creek trestle on the Waycross Air Line Saturday. He was on his engine and as he reached the trestle, he saw a light the size of the headlight of a locomotive, swinging across the track at the center of the trestle. He and his fireman thought they were running into danger and the engine was reversed. As soon as the engine stopped, the light quickly disappeared. It is said that others have seen strange sights at the same place. The cause of the phenomena is not known. Alvin said that he was alarmed by the light and was afraid it was a sign of danger.

August 1894
Ocmulgee Mounds, Bibb County, Central Georgia

Aug 9, 1894 - The Macon Telegraph (Macon, Bibb County, GA)

OVER THE RIVER IN EAST MACON

The Colored People Badly Wrought Up Over a Somewhat Strange Phenomenon.

WAS IT A JACK O' LANTERN?

The negroes in East Macon are very much worked up over a strange phenomenon that they claim made its appearance on Fort Hill some nights ago. A large party of colored men got together with all the dogs in the neighborhood for a coon hunt, and early in the evening started out for the river swamp. It was after the hunt, when the party started home, that they were badly frightened by something of the "jack o' lantern" kind, and which has stirred their superstitious natures to a point of great excitement.

They spent nearly the whole night hunting and were returning home with a very good bag, when, just as they reached the Indian mound beyond the railroad, a large, faint light was seen on the summit of the hand-made mountain. It would move about as if carried by some one and passed from one side of the mound to the other, going each time to the edge and at times appearing to swing some distance down the side. It was too large and too faint for a lantern. It is described as being the size of a Japanese lantern, though the light was red, rather than yellow.

All sorts of conjectures arose as to what the phenomenon could be. Some of the negroes believed it to be the risen spirit of some Indians who searched for the buried relics that are found from time to time in the mound, a goodly collection of which has already been made by many people in the neighborhood. Some of the men became frightened and beat a hasty retreat. One or two wanted to investigate, and with this determination clambered up the side of the mound, their minds made up to risk life if necessary to satisfy their curiosity.

They say that when they approached near enough to the top to get a view all over its surface the mysterious light was seen half hidden behind a clump of bushes on the opposite side from which they approached. It was as large as a water bucket and was so dim as not to throw any noticeable light upon the ground around it.

The men, there were three of them, as soon as they reached the top made a bold rush toward the "thing." It was too quick for them, however, and, seeming to divine their purpose, rose up with a weird hissing noise and floated heavenward with all the gracefulness of an infant balloon, leaving the awe-struck darkies almost paralyzed in their boots.

They stood there watching it until from the diminished size of a baseball it passed out of view. It is needless to say that the dauntless explorers never lost any time on the mound searching for tracks or other signs, but with all the haste at their command they tumbled head first down the side of the mound, evidently more eager to get away from those parts than they had been a few minutes before to ferret out the mystery.

Of course, the story as told by them is not to be credited. But that they saw something of the kind and they are very badly wrought up over whatever it was there can be no doubt.

Some of the young men of East Macon proposed yesterday to watch for the appearance of the phenomenon last night and the result of their vigil may develop an ever more sensational story than that given out by the colored people.

November 1896
Tennille, Washington County, Central Georgia

Nov 16, 1896 - The Constitution (Atlanta, Fulton County, GA)

There appears to be some truth in the recent mysterious light story on the Washington and Tennille railroad. Mr. Carson Lanier, the engineer, first discovered a strange light only a short distance ahead of his engine on the track, which caused him to slow up, he thinking it was another train just ahead. The light then disappeared and again showed up a short distance in the rear of the train on which Mr. Lanier had charge. The mysterious light appeared to outtravel his train, which was going at the rate of about nine miles an hour. The passengers' attention was attracted by the strange light, but no satisfactory account could be given as to the cause of it. Mr. Lanier says that his colored trainman, Fayte, became very much frightened and seemed to think the world was coming to an end.

January 1898
Rome, Floyd County, Northwest Georgia

Nov 16, 1898 - The Atlanta Journal (Atlanta, Fulton County, GA)

A mysterious blue light passed over Rome Thursday night.

June 1905
Sylvania, Screven County, Southeast Georgia

Jun 25, 1905 - The Constitution (Atlanta, Fulton County, GA)

STRANGE LIGHT IS SEEN IN SKY NEAR SYLVANIA

SYLVANIA, GA., June 24.—(Special.) R. R. Mock, of Sylvania, and Mr. Vandeville, of Atlanta, were witnesses of a very peculiar and startling celestial phenomenon on Wednesday night of this week. They were driving in from a country trip about 10 miles above Sylvania, when, just before 1 o'clock in the morning, they perceived a bright light coming up above the horizon in the east, as if it was a very large star. The waning moon was then some distance up in the sky. Mr. Mock remarked that it was the largest star he has ever seen and his companion laughed and said that it was the top of a tree on fire some distance away. Directly, however, the strange light rose higher and they both saw then that it was in the sky and not of the earth; it appeared to the two men about the shape and size of an old field stump on fire and the light would flash out on each side occasionally and then go back. Gradually it rose higher, apparently at about the same rate as the other heavenly bodies, for they noticed that it remained at about the same distance from the moon all the time. At times it looked like a large lantern hung in the heavens and assumed different shapes until at last it became round like a full moon and as large and bright. Both the gentlemen declare that the light from the strange body lighted up all the trees in the woods through which they were driving. They watched it intently until they arrived at Sylvania, about 3 o'clock in the morning, when they aroused a number of the citizens, who got up and looked at it; it then appeared to be several times as large as the largest star and was some distance up in the sky. Once or twice while they were gazing at it, it would disappear from view for a minute or two and would then reappear. It was an absolutely clear night and there was not a cloud in the sky. The strange visitor was watched intently until approaching day obscured its sight and shut it out from view.

This curious phenomenon has aroused much interest among the people here, who would like for the astronomers to tell them exactly what it was. Of course, it is generally supposed that it was a meteor of some kind, but it acted very differently and took its course with more deliberation than those erratic visitors usually do. It has been suggested that it might have been an illuminated balloon of some kind that was up in the air that night, but this theory is scouted at by those who saw it, for they say it would have been impossible for any balloon to have cast such a bright light at such a distance as this body did. The moon, they say, although shining with more than half of its disc illuminated paled before this strange rival. Whatever it might have been, it is true that it was there in the heavens that night. It was seen by a number of reliable citizens of our town and looked and moved as has been described.

September 1911
Atlanta, Fulton County, Capital Region

Sept 17, 1911 - The Atlanta Journal (Atlanta, Fulton County, GA)

MYSTERIOUS LIGHT IN THE EAST PUZZLES CITIZENS AND VANISHES

A new star arose above the firmament somewhere between Decatur and Atlanta last night shortly after 9 o'clock. It came into view suddenly, as red as Mephisto when he sprang from the pit of fire. For an instant it paused in mid-air as if hesitating which way to go. Then, like a homing pigeon, it headed for Atlanta.

It was particularly plain to watchers in Druid Hills and along Highland avenue. Slowly and majestically the huge, fiery "thing" came toward the city.

A stray dog glimpsed the mystery, sat on his haunches and yelped plaintively. Attracted by this a group of children playing in the street became frightened and rushed indoors. An extremely temperate youth who had taken only one glass, feared to ask his companion if he, too, saw the "thing:" a superstitious negro took it as a dreadful warning and began to chant a prayer, and family groups gazed at the approaching light and at each other, fearing to speak their thoughts.

The "thing" gained speed. It seemed to spread out over the whole eastern sky. The eyes of the watchers became filled with a red glare, dotted with the spots one sees when gazing squarely at the sun. They were blinded for fully a moment. Then, gradually, all cleared, and only the blue-black sky, specked with stars, could be seen.

May 1917
Americus, Sumter County, Southwest Georgia

May 11, 1917 - The Americus Times-Recorder (Americus, Sumter County, GA)

There is a mysterious light on Mt. Alto which flashes nightly near Rome. Just a call to arms.

July 1922
Oaky Ridge, Habersham County, Northeast Georgia

July 27, 1922 - The Monroe Advertiser (Forysth, Monroe County, GA)

MYSTERIOUS LIGHTS ON MOUNTAIN TOP

WHAT IS THOUGHT TO BE AN ELABORATE SYSTEM TO WARN MOONSHINERS OF DANGER IS SEEN AT CLARKESVILLE

CLARKESVILLE, Ga.—Mysterious lights, believed to be operated by moonshiners as an elaborate signal system, have set the citizens of this town agog with excited curiosity for the past week.

Beginning shortly after dark and continuing for hours, half a dozen or more of the lights wink their signals from the inky blackness of Oaky Ridge mountain, ten miles north of Clarkesville. Questions to residents of the vicinity of Oaky Ridge elicits nothing more than a stony silence, and officers are baffled in their efforts to locate the lights or discover their meaning.

According to a prominent Clarkesville citizen, who staid up most of Friday night watching the strange lights, there is one master station, apparently a powerful searchlight sending its code messages by means of shutters. Immediately after the start of the master light, half a dozen other lights, separated by miles of ridge and forest, begin their answering winks.

Shortly before midnight Friday, and immediately after the apparent stop of transmission by the master station, a star shell, resembling the shells fired from the Verry pistols, used as trench signals during the war, answered from far down the valley. Three shells were fired into the air. There was an immediate answering signal from stations on the mountain, and for fifteen minutes the mountain seemed alive with twinkling lights.

Suggestions made by several persons that a party be organized to go to the mountains for the purpose of ascertaining the meaning of the lights, have received little encouragement.

Oaky Ridge is a long "hog-back" range, running from east to west, and is some ten or twelve miles long. It is very inaccessible, and only a few persons live on the mountain, which is known as a favorite place for the operation of illicit whiskey stills.

December 1923
Macon, Bibb County, Central Georgia

Dec 21, 1923 - The Macon News (Macon, Bibb County, GA)

Have You Seen Mystery Light? Two Men Have

A mystery is a mystery, the same as nails is nails, and pigs is pigs, though all of them may be, and often are, very simple when explained.

Anyway a certain Macon man has for the past few weeks at intervals been seeing a strange light in the sky at about the time in the evening that window shades and the shades of night begin to come down that has had him wondering if perhaps the time had come to 'lighten' up on the drinks, or whether the strange glitter heavenward was discernible to others.

The man in question saw the light first about three weeks ago and last night about seven o'clock standing on a front porch at a home on Cherry street and looking South he saw it again. This time he had a witness who saw it also, which, he said, encourages him in the belief that he may yet safely continue to be a member of the "We Won't Go Home Until Morning Club."

Of course it may be an aeroplane light, or a balloon light, or some other kind of natural light, but after all its a light, the man said, and until further "enlightened" in the matter he concluded his observations by remarking that at best it was a darn bad night last night for an aeroplane or any other kind of vehicle to be out rambling around either on earth or in the clouds.

Chapter 4: Celestial Strangeness

February 1872
Raytown, Taliaferro County, East Georgia

Feb 8, 1872 - The Daily Sun (Atlanta, Fulton County, GA)

A Sign in the Heavens—What Was It?

Raytown, Ga., February 5, 1872.

Editors of the Sun: One of the most remarkable and wonderful phenomena ever noticed before was witnessed in this vicinity last night. It was a red appearance of the sky covering a considerable space just a little North of East. Its lower verge was about 20 degrees above the horizon, and its upper about 40. It was about as wide as it was long. Its form was not regular; its greatest length extending from the Southeast to the Northwest. It was first noticed at about 8 o'clock, P.M., and looked very much like the light of a great fire at a distance, reflected from the clouds, of a cloudy night. But last night was perfectly clear and the stars were shining brightly.

The strange light soon turned to a blood red. It had none of the appearance of what is called "Northern lights;" there were no streaks or shooting up rays. It seemed to be perfectly still, the only visible changes being a lessening and then an increasing of the deep crimson color.

At the same time there was noticed in another part of the heavens, off to the Northwest, another, something like an indistinct, or not well defined comet.

Both these strange lights were seen until about 10 o'clock, when they passed away.

I understand that the same lights, or strange sights in the heavens, were seen at Washington, Crawfordville and Barnett. Can any one tell what they were? or whether any thing like them has ever been seen before?

Enquirer.

May 1874
Savannah, Chatham County, Southeast Georgia

June 19, 1874 - The Morning News (Savannah, Chatham County, GA)

Meteors.—Unusually bright meteors have been reported on the following dates: The 8th, 10th, 14th, 16th, 17th, 18th, 19th, 20th, 21st, and 25th.

June 1875
Lincolnton, Lincoln County, East Georgia

June 5, 1875 - The Daily Constitutionalist (Augusta, Richmond County, GA)

Some strange sights have been seen in the heavens throughout this section. About a month or six weeks since, what appeared to be large ball of fire was seen by several persons in the western sky about sundown, and before it disappeared, it seemed to burst into a thousand pieces. Did not see it myself, but suppose it must have been a meteor. And again, last week, after sunrise, a gentleman whose word will stand, states that he saw near the sun, a black spot very much resembling a coffin, and it remained for some time, when it disappeared, and then two very bright stars were seen, which remained visible for an hour or more. Several other persons saw the stars. Mr. Editor, we are not given much to signs, &c., but we would like to know something of these singular scenes in the heavens.

March 1877
Conyers, Rockdale County, Capital Region

Mar 11, 1877 - The Atlanta Daily Constitution (Atlanta, Fulton County, GA)

The Conyers Courier says that on last Tuesday night about half past eight o'clock, as Mr. Chas. McAlister was returning home, he witnessed a phenomenal event which merits a brief description. A large round body of light darted downward from a northeast direction, and when apparently a short distance from the earth, a smaller ball of light ran horizontally until the two came together. There was no explosion, but a sudden burst of blue lights which illuminated the scene for about a minute. Mr. McAlister describes the phenomenon as one of surpassing beauty.

February 1895
Clarkesville, Habersham County, Northeast Georgia

Feb 28, 1895 - The Toccoa Times (Toccoa, Stephens County, GA)

The Star Dances.

To the Editor of The Times:

Not long since I was visiting a friend when something very queer and almost unreasonable came to my notice. About 8 o'clock at night the gentleman of the house walked out on the piazza and seemed to be viewing the horizon for a few minutes, and suddenly he said, "Ray, did you ever see the dancing star?" "The dancing devil," I exclaimed. "Yes," said he, "there is actually a star in the South, yonder, that dances from place to place." Now, I would not have believed this if the President had said it, if I had not seen it. But, when I went to look myself I had to believe it. There it was, quite a bright star, due south, and it would move first to the right, then to the left, then up, and then down. Seeing is believing, and as I said before, if I had not have seen it myself I should not have believed it.

No doubt some will say that "he has seen a hob goblin;" well now I have seen hob goblins all my life, but I never saw a star before that danced.

To see this star one must get on high ground, and look south. I don't want any one to say I have lied until they have sufficiently tested the matter. It is plainly visible, when the sky is clear, from the residence of C. H. Sutton, Clarkesville; or at the residence of T. T. Jones, Azalea.

Ray, Azalea, Ga., Feb. 26.

June 1897
Warrenton, Warren County, East Georgia

June 19, 1897 - The Morning News (Savannah, Chatham County, GA)

METEOR AT WARRENTON

Citizens Who Thought They Saw the Airship.

Warrenton, Ga., June 17.—Last night, about 8 o'clock, the people here were excited by a sudden and brilliant lighting up of the earth and sky, as a large meteor flashed by. It passed along in the north, disappearing in the west. To-day some of the some of the citizens claim to see something floating in the air, which they variously denominate airship, meteor, star, etc.

February 1898
Stephens Atoms, Oglethorpe County, East Georgia

Feb 19, 1898 - The Semi-Weekly Echo (Crawford, Oglethorpe County, GA)

Capt W. L. Johnson was the first to discover the dancing star now visible in the south clear evenings.

August 1908
Macon, Bibb County, Central Georgia

Aug 23, 1908 - The Macon Daily Telegraph (Macon, Bibb County, GA)

BRIGHT STAR WAS TWINKLING IN THE HEAVENS AT NOONTIME

UNUSUAL SIGHT WITNESSED BY MANY—DISCOVERED BY INDUSTRIOUS STAR GAZER SHORTLY AFTER 12 O'CLOCK.

Some industrious star-gazer browsing about the vicinity of Cherry and Third streets yesterday shortly after noon discovered a star twinkling in the southwestern heavens.

The star-gazer told his neighbor and the neighbor told his neighbor and within a very few minutes this business section of the city was converted into an open-air observatory, crowds of people congregating with necks strained skyward and eyes blinking in the brilliant sunshine.

The star was a mere speck in the ocean of ether, though distinctly visible to the naked eye after once discovered but many sought it without success, and the skeptics who were unable to locate the stellar speck that had dared to work overtime walked away in disgust, declaring that it was all a joke and a public hoax. There were some who wanted to find the man who started the "joke," after they had gotten cricks in their necks, but he had been lost in the multitude of "original discoverers."

It was amusing to watch the eager searchers who scanned the heavens diligently, unable to locate the elusive planet for some time, and then study the expression of victory depicted on their faces in the moment of success. A glimpse beyond the pearly gates of the Eternal city could hardly have produced a smile of greater satisfaction. A nearby real estate agent found an old pair of binoculars and these were soon in general use, while others prepared pieces of smoked glass, through which they could more easily contemplate the beauty of the one single, innocent star that had evidently overslept its work hours and had aroused itself in confusion, and was now trying to perform its daily task, though its services were not in demand.

Negroes of the more ignorant class and a swarthy foreigner who sold ice cream cakes "five fer da nick," looked on the phenomenon as an ill omen and moved about with solemn faces, making timid inquiries of their white friends as to what it might portend.

Those of a philosophic turn of mind took a deep interest in studying the busy little twinkler from a student's point of view, while others of a sentimental temperament were wrapped in admiration of the brave fight the tiny fellow was making against the great bright sun that was aggressively advancing on him along the broad highway of heaven. During the afternoon heavy clouds assembled and the star disappeared.

The appearance of stars during the day time is not unusual, it is said, by those familiar with astronomy, but it is not often that they are discovered by busy people hurrying along the streets of Macon.

October 1909
Macon, Bibb County, Central Georgia

Oct 5, 1909 - The Macon Daily Telegraph (Macon, Bibb County, GA)

LIGHT OF NEW COMET VISIBLE LAST NIGHT

Peculiar Phenomenon of the Skies Attracted Attention of Many

A curious, intermittently appearing streak of white light, its intensity much like the glow or reflection from a fire, but looking, too, as if it might be the product of a gigantic vari-colored searchlight, amazed and mystified hundreds of local observers of the heavens last night.

By many the phenomenon was accredited to be Halley's comet, the much-talked of solar body that, after a lapse of over seventy years, is again making its appearance in the heavens. There being no professional astronomers in Macon, this belief could not be verified, and those interested had to content themselves with merely looking and wondering.

About 8:30 o'clock reports came to The Telegraph office of a big fire, the location of which was differently given by various people, all of whom stated that they had seen the reflection in the sky. Diligent investigation failed to locate any fire, either in the city, the outskirts or in the nearby rural districts. Observation was then made from the roof of the American National Bank building and the source of all the reports was soon sighted. It appeared at irregular intervals, this flash, in the lower northwestern part of the heavens not greatly above the horizon, and its light was of a subdued brilliance. For a minute it would look exactly like the tail of a comet, which, however, is of only momentary duration, and then, as it began to fade, the colors would glow and succeed each other in some sort of shimmering waves or changes. Sometimes it would only be a few minutes between the appearance of this spectacle, again the periods would be at least fifteen minutes in length.

All of the janitors and elevator workers of the American National, Commercial National and other buildings gathered on the roofs and watched the peculiar and unusual sight for hours, their interest growing with each appearance and disappearance of the supposed comet's light. The negroes not being at all familiar with the affairs of the solar systems marveled at the attraction, like "watchers of the skies, when a new star swims into their ken," and many and varied were their conjectures.

The heavens will doubtless be watched tonight with eager interest by hundreds of readers of The Telegraph.

January 1910
Rome, Floyd County, Northwest Georgia

Feb 1, 1910 - The Atlanta Semi-Weekly Journal (Atlanta, Fulton County, GA)

VENUS FADES, REAPPEARS IN PUZZLING MANNER

Amateur Astronomers See a Strange Sight in Sky, Watching for Comet

ROME, Ga., Jan. 28.—While looking for the new comet a party of amateur Rome astronomers observed a sight that caused them no little wonderment. The planet Venus was seen to fade away and reappear at frequent intervals, from 6 until 7 o'clock. Then it resumed its steady beam.

Members of the sky-gazing party are willing to take affidavit that this really happened last night.

July 1913
Atlanta, Fulton County, Capital Region

July 17, 1913 - The Atlanta Georgian (Atlanta, Fulton County, GA)

Hundreds See Red Star, Mystery to Sky Students, Fall

Astronomers and hundreds of Atlantans who delight in gazing at the moon were treated to a peculiar and awe-inspiring spectacle about 9 o'clock Wednesday night.

For several nights there had been seen two beautiful stars close to the moon. One was brilliant and perfectly white. Its position in the early part of the night was above the moon, just a little to the left. The other was of ruby color, very brilliant. It was above the moon, just a little to the right.

Wednesday night at the hour mentioned, the red star began to move, slowly but distinctly, in a southwesterly direction, gradually falling until it vanished just above the horizon.

It was about ten minutes from the time this star began its descent until it vanished.

August 1918
Atlanta, Fulton County, Capital Region

Aug 12, 1918 - The Atlanta Georgian (Atlanta, Fulton County, GA)

Believes Allies Right After Seeing Star of Red, White and Blue

There no longer is any doubt in the mind of this American, of German descent, as to which side is in the right of the great war.

J. H. Bartenfield, of Center Hill, was coming home from church Sunday night when he saw a most mysterious phenomena in the Western sky. It was a star that appeared to him first red, then white, then blue. He called out members of his family, on reaching his home, and they, too, saw the strange sight.

"I feel that the star was a sign of God showing me the right in the terrible conflict across the seas," said Mr. Bartenfield Monday. "My parents were natives of Germany and at first my natural inclinations were for that country, but since America entered the war I had undergone a change of mind. If there was any further doubt whatever in my mind as to which side I should irrevocably commit myself and all my energies it was removed last night when I saw that red, white and blue star."

Chapter 5: Other Anomalies

September 1862
Grooverville, Brooks County, Southwest Georgia

Sept 29, 1862 - The Countryman (Turnwold, Putnam County, GA)

A Phenomenon—Sword in the Heavens

"We are informed by gentlemen whose veracity cannot be questioned, that on the 23d ult., near Grooverville, Georgia, a phenomenon was witnessed in the heavens, at about 4 o'clock in the evening. It was a perfect representation of a sword—handle, blade and point all visible. The blade was red, and the handle silver color. The blade pointed to the northeast, and the handle to the southwest. It was high up in the heavens, appearing to the eye to be about twenty feet long, and two feet broad. Soon after it was witnessed, a wind springing up, heavy clouds appeared, and screened it from view.

We are not one of those who attach a peculiar significance to remarkable dreams, believe in witchcraft, or view every celestial phenomenon as an omen of good or evil. But no similar phenomenon to the one in question has been witnessed for many generations, and we are, therefore, owing to the peculiar circumstances surrounding us, inclined to regard it as significant.

Flavius Josephus, in his history of the Jews, refers to s similar appearance in the heavens just previous to the destruction of Jerusalem. He says that a star, resembling a sword, stood over the city, and a comet that continued a whole year. Another writer, we are informed, describes the sword as hanging over the city with the point down.

After the destruction of Jerusalem, the star disappeared. This phenomenon has always, by learned divines, been described as the

"Sword of the Lord." From the destruction of Jerusalem to the present period, no such representation has been beheld in the heavens."

The above is copied from the Family Friend of Monticello, Fla., in order to show what folly and fanaticism exist, even in our day.

July 1875
Greensboro, Greene County, East Georgia

July 27, 1875 - The Georgia Weekly Telegraph and Journal & Messenger (Macon, Bibb County, GA)

Under the head of "Strange Phenomenon," the Greensboro Herald prints the following:

We are having many very remarkable phenomena in nature. Last Thursday evening several of our citizens heard a singular rumbling noise, directly over head in the heavens, like the sound of a distant train of cars or the running of a threshing machine. The noise continued without intermission for over two hours. Not a cloud was discernable in the whole range of vision.

July 1881
Americus, Sumter County, Southwest Georgia

July 15, 1881 - The Savannah Morning News (Savannah, Chatham County, GA)

Americus Republican: "Mr. Z. T. Baisden gives us the following story of a whirlwind that visited his place about 12 o'clock on Monday, scaring all his hands and some visitors very badly: A whirlwind occurred in a twelve acre corn field that was about four feet in diameter and sometimes a hundred feet high. The body of it was perfectly black, with fire in centre, and emitted a strong sulphurous vapor that could be smelt three hundred yards from it. The whirlwind would divide into three, and move rapidly over the field twisting up the corn stalks by the roots and carrying them up. These three minor whirlwinds would then come together with a loud crash, cracking and burning, and shoot high up into the heavens. Three young ladies who were visiting Mrs. Baisden, went in about one hundred and fifty feet to observe it, but received such a shower of burning sand upon their faces and necks, that they ran affrighted to the house. Mr. Baisden says that he cannot account for this strange phenomenon, and it certainly frightened all who saw it. The strange part was that it contained fire, yet did not appear to burn the corn that it did not tear up, and its sulphurous vapor that sickened and burnt all who got close enough to get a full breath of it."

June 1887
Columbus, Muskogee County, West Georgia

June 11, 1887 - The Valdosta Times (Valdosta, Lowndes County, GA)

A Big Black Cloud.

Columbus Ledger.

Mr. A. M. Christian, who resides six miles from the city, in this county, tells of a strange phenomenon witnessed in his neighborhood day before yesterday.

During the afternoon, an immense black cloud gathered, and instead of floating overhead, descended to the earth, withering everything with which it came in contact. The cloud was sufficiently large to cover a twenty acre field of cotton, every stalk immediately drooped, and the field will have to be replanted.

The cloud arose and settled upon the farm of Mr. John L. Willis, where it scorched and destroyed about ten acres of corn.

It arose and fell as it moved along before the wind in a southeasterly direction, and everywhere it touched the earth it blighted trees and grass and growing crops alike. It killed fifteen acres of cotton for Mr. Joe Brooks, five for Mr. Will Brittain and many other farmers were injured. The cloud must have been heavily charged with electricity.

June 1897
Acworth, Cobb County, Capital Region

June 14, 1897 - The Atlanta Journal (Atlanta, Fulton County, GA)

WORSE THAN THE AIR SHIP.—It is reported that a strange looking figure which resembled a woman with long floating hair was seen by a few of our citizens a few evenings ago, flying through the air three or four hundred feet over the Litchfield hotel.—Acworth Post

July 1898
Atlanta, Fulton County, Capital Region

July 7, 1898 - The Constitution (Atlanta, Fulton County, GA)

THE PICTURE OF CUBA SEEN IN THE CLOUDS.

It is not altogether from a study of the Bible that the story of phenomena is found, for even in these days of war when there are no King Belshazzars to read the handwriting on the wall, there are strange things to be seen.

Late yesterday afternoon a curious phenomenon appeared in the southern sky, where, wrapped in the clouds, was outlined the island of Cuba as plainly as it is outlined on the map. The island, in every line; in its hills and mountains, bays and rivers, was perfectly traced in the clouds. There were the shadows and lights and curves and corners and to those who had studied the map the island was plainly discernible.

Many saw the strange picture in the clouds and there were many who looked intently at the island. A car going to Decatur was filled with passengers and at an abrupt turn in the track the painting blazed in all its beauty and symmetry upon the gaze of the astonished passengers.

Everybody on the car saw it and the car was stopped so that a better look could be secured. Mr. E. H. Carter, of the Meridian cotton mills of Mississippi, was one to see the island.

"It was absolutely perfect," he said. "There was the bay of Havana, the bay of Santiago and the various inlets that are to be found on the map. It was as perfect as could be found in the geographies and as plain as if printed in ink on fine paper."

"The picture was perfect in its outlines," said Mr. J. H. Smythe, "and the execution of the lines, shadows and indentations along the coast could not have been excelled by a draftsman. I never saw anything in my life more plain. Above the cloud of island fell the light of the moon and the picture was one of marvelous beauty and grandeur."

All over the city the strange phenomenon was commented upon. From Broad street bridge an excellent view could be secured and from the tall office buildings the scene was wonderfully beautiful and sublime. The picture in the clouds remained several minutes before it vanished.

October 1903
Valdosta, Lowndes County, South Georgia

Oct 17, 1903 - The Valdosta Times (Valdosta, Lowndes County, GA)

SHE MAKES THE STAR "GO OUT."

A Negro Woman Who is Creating Something of a Sensation in Valdosta.

The colored camp meeting at Pine park has gone on with unabated interest this week, the attendance each night being very large. It is expected that next Sunday will witness the greatest crowds of the entire meeting.

A sensational feature among those who have attended the meetings is a woman named Sarah Holland, who was brought to the meetings by Bishop Lomax and who professes to have extra power from on high. She says she has seen bright lights in the skies and has heard voices of unseen hosts swarming about her. She claims to have communion with the spirit world and have power to heal the sick, as well. She also claims to be able to make the brightest star disappear from view, and she has given several seances during the week.

On Tuesday night she had a large crowd of negroes, in pain and distress, about her, seeking relief. Each of them testified that she or he had found relief, but finally one negro man said he was not certain whether he was relieved or not. He was suffering with the toothache. The woman did not like his reply, so she told them that he did not have sense enough to know whether he was well or not.

The same night she gave an exhibition of making the "star go out" to a large crowd in the rear of the grandstand. A number of white men were on hand to witness it. The negroes say that she picked out one of the brightest stars in the sky and told them to keep their eyes upon it. Then they sang a few songs and said a few prayers and the star disappeared from view. After remaining out of sight a few minutes, the spell was broken and the star came back.

The woman is a native of North Carolina and she has made a great impression upon the negroes who have heard her talk and seen her wonderful works. It was announced yesterday that she would give another exhibition of "putting out the star" tonight, and a big crowd will probably be on hand to witness the event.

December 1906
Gum Swamp, Telfair County, South Georgia

Jan 11, 1907 - The Dahlonega Nugget (Dahlonega, Lumpkin County, GA)

A Strange Phenomenon.

Several have told us this week of what they consider a very strange freak of nature in the hammock on Gum Swamp about five miles from here. It is found opposite the place of Mr. Tucker Browning and was discovered a few weeks ago. There is a spot there, so our informant tells us, where it rains all the time and that when the sun shines it rains harder than when cloudy. The water that falls has a salty taste also and the people who have visited this place cannot account for the strange phenomenon that seems to exist there.—Telfair Enterprise.

February 1908
Atlanta, Fulton County, Capital Region

Feb 10, 1908 - The Atlanta Georgian and News (Atlanta, Fulton County, GA)

STRANGE LIGHT IN HEAVENS PRECEDED SNOW STORM

A strange phenomenon was seen in the sky Sunday morning at 3 o'clock by policemen who were on duty at that hour, and they think it may have had some bearing on the sleet storm.

Policemen Bullard and Gillespie, who were standing near the corner of Decatur and Courtland-sts., at this hour, were attracted by a sudden and brilliant light in the heavens, and got a good view of the phenomenon. In describing the sight, the officers stated that the sky was illuminated by a streak of flame apparently 10 feet in length and 1 foot in width.

"This flaming light was stationary," said the officers, "and never once moved from its position. It remained in the sky for fully twenty minutes, after which it began to gradually fade away. This continued slowly until finally the whole of the light had vanished."

"I have seen meteors," said Officer Bullard, "but never before have I seen such a peculiar sight, as this in the heavens. As we watched the strange light, I told Mr. Gillespie that something unusual would follow. I am satisfied this phenomenon was connected in some way with the sleet storm."

Also by Erin Cain

Georgia Wildmen: Exploring the History of Relict Hominoids in the
Peach State
Mysteries Over Georgia

Watch for more at https://www.erin-cain.com.